The CAMPING JOURNAL of

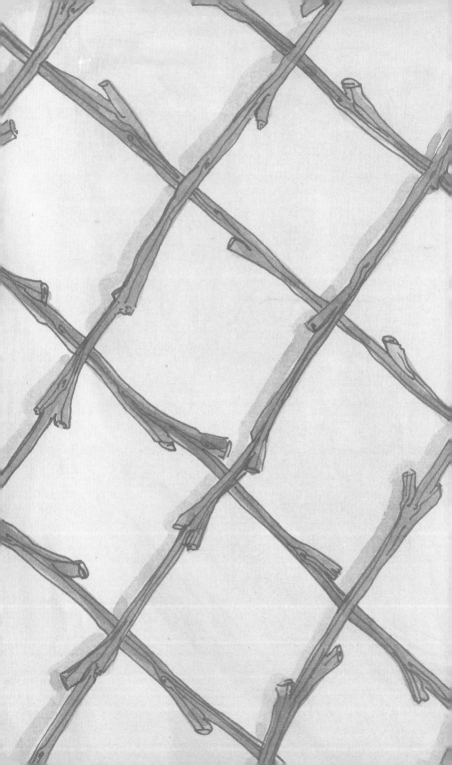

CONTENTS

YOUR CAMPING JOURNAL

Enjoying the beautiful outdoors with friends and family is one of the greatest pleasures in life.

We barbecue in our backyards, look for restaurants that allow us to dine alfresco, and picnic by the beach, all with the same purpose…to delight in this beautiful place we call home.

From the humble backpacker to the glamorous RV camper, everyone appreciates the joy of being in nature. Camping—no matter your shelter, no matter your age—has become one of our most beloved pastimes. This journal is chock-full of clever DIY ideas, delicious recipes, and useful information to make your camping experience one to remember. You'll find comprehensive checklists to keep you organized and special camping detail pages in which you can record important camping activities as well as the memories made along the way. Because a day of camping is never complete without a campfire sing-along, you'll find a nostalgic and engaging song you and your friends and family can enjoy together. (Remember "Father Abraham"?) You'll even find a place for your favorite photos. So hit the road or hit the trail. Your adventure in nature is waiting for you!

CAMP CHECKLISTS

CAMP KITCHEN CHECKLIST

- [ ] Barbecue tongs, forks, spatulas, skewers
- [ ] Bottle opener, can opener, corkscrew
- [ ] Cups, plates, bowls, platters
- [ ] Cutting boards
- [ ] Dishpan
- [ ] Foil, zippered plastic bags
- [ ] Food storage containers
- [ ] French press, milk frother
- [ ] Kettle
- [ ] Knives
- [ ] Mixing bowls
- [ ] Napkins, tablecloth, dishtowels
- [ ] Pots and pans
- [ ] Pot holders, oven mitts
- [ ] Silverware
- [ ] Sponges, dish soap
- [ ] Stirring and serving spoons
- [ ] Strainer
- [ ] Vegetable peeler

CAMP TOOLS CHECKLIST

- [ ] Air pump
- [ ] Ax, hatchet
- [ ] Bungee cords, rope, clothespins
- [ ] Camp stove, charcoal
- [ ] Candles, lantern
- [ ] Chairs, table
- [ ] Compass, solar phone charger
- [ ] Duct tape
- [ ] Fire extinguisher
- [ ] First aid kit, bug spray
- [ ] Matches, lighter
- [ ] Scissors
- [ ] Shovel
- [ ] Tarps
- [ ] Tissues, paper towels, toilet paper, wipes
- [ ] Tool kit, sewing kit
- [ ] Trash bags

CAMP FOOD CHECKLIST

- [ ] Boxed milk, juice boxes, water
- [ ] Boxed soup
- [ ] Bread
- [ ] Condiments
- [ ] Cooking oil, cooking spray
- [ ] Dried pasta, sauce
- [ ] Eggs, butter, cheese
- [ ] Graham crackers, marshmallows, chocolate
- [ ] Granola, cereal
- [ ] Ground coffee, tea bags, hot chocolate packets
- [ ] Instant oatmeal
- [ ] Meats
- [ ] Pancake mix, syrup, honey
- [ ] Peanut butter, jelly
- [ ] Popcorn, snacks, pretzels
- [ ] Salt, pepper, spices, dried herbs
- [ ] Veggies, fruit

ALL THE EXTRAS CHECKLIST

- ☐ Activity books
- ☐ Art journal, watercolor pencils, paints
- ☐ Batteries
- ☐ Board games, cards, books
- ☐ Book light
- ☐ Books on constellations, flora, and fauna
- ☐ Inflatable mattress
- ☐ iPod, music
- ☐ Paper, pencils, pens
- ☐ Roll-up outdoor mat
- ☐ Sheets, blankets, pillows
- ☐ String lights
- ☐ Towels (bath, hand, beach)
- ☐ Umbrella (sun, rain)
- ☐ Vase or jar for flowers

DATE: _____ LOCATION: _____

CAMPGROUND: _____ PHONE: _____

SITE #/ CABIN #: _____ COST PER NIGHT: _____

AMENITIES: _____

ELECTRIC: _____ WATER: _____ RESTROOMS: _____

WEATHER: _____

CAMPING COMPANIONS: _____
_____
_____

BEST MEALS: _____
_____
_____

FAVORITE MEMORIES: _____
_____
_____
_____

ADVENTURES AND SITES VISITED: _____
_____
_____

DATE: _____ LOCATION: _____

CAMPGROUND: _____ PHONE: _____

SITE #/ CABIN #: _____ COST PER NIGHT: _____

AMENITIES: _____

ELECTRIC: _____ WATER: _____ RESTROOMS: _____

WEATHER: _____

CAMPING COMPANIONS: _____
_____
_____

BEST MEALS: _____
_____
_____

FAVORITE MEMORIES: _____
_____
_____
_____

ADVENTURES AND SITES VISITED: _____
_____
_____

DATE: _____ LOCATION: _____

CAMPGROUND: _____ PHONE: _____

SITE #/ CABIN #: _____ COST PER NIGHT: _____

AMENITIES: _____

ELECTRIC: _____ WATER: _____ RESTROOMS: _____

WEATHER: _____

CAMPING COMPANIONS: _____

_____

_____

BEST MEALS: _____

_____

_____

FAVORITE MEMORIES: _____

_____

_____

_____

ADVENTURES AND SITES VISITED: _____

_____

_____

DATE: _____ LOCATION: _____

CAMPGROUND: _____ PHONE: _____

SITE #/ CABIN #: _____ COST PER NIGHT: _____

AMENITIES: _____

ELECTRIC: _____ WATER: _____ RESTROOMS: _____

WEATHER: _____

CAMPING COMPANIONS: _____

_____

_____

BEST MEALS: _____

_____

_____

FAVORITE MEMORIES: _____

_____

_____

_____

ADVENTURES AND SITES VISITED: _____

_____

_____

DATE: _____ LOCATION: _____

CAMPGROUND: _____ PHONE: _____

SITE #/ CABIN #: _____ COST PER NIGHT: _____

AMENITIES: _____

ELECTRIC: _____ WATER: _____ RESTROOMS: _____

WEATHER: _____

CAMPING COMPANIONS: _____

_____

_____

BEST MEALS: _____

_____

_____

FAVORITE MEMORIES: _____

_____

_____

_____

ADVENTURES AND SITES VISITED: _____

_____

_____

DATE: _____ LOCATION: _____

CAMPGROUND: _____ PHONE: _____

SITE #/ CABIN #: _____ COST PER NIGHT: _____

AMENITIES: _____

ELECTRIC: _____ WATER: _____ RESTROOMS: _____

WEATHER: _____

CAMPING COMPANIONS: _____
_____
_____

BEST MEALS: _____
_____
_____

FAVORITE MEMORIES: _____
_____
_____
_____

ADVENTURES AND SITES VISITED: _____
_____
_____

I am with you
and will watch over you
wherever you go.

GENESIS 28:15

FIRST AID

CAMP FIRST AID KIT

Camping in nature can be a fun and rewarding experience. Being aware of a few plants and knowing some easy all-natural remedies can make all the difference regarding your adventure. A well-stocked first aid kit and a sharp eye are two ways to ensure you enjoy your time outdoors!

ibuprofen

allergy medicine

Pepto

antacid

ice pack

alcohol wipes

bandage

nail clippers

scissors

Band-Aids

safety pins

first aid cream

Neosporin

Q-tips

tweezers

peroxide

D.I.Ys
PAIN RELIEVERS AND
ALL-NATURAL BUG SPRAYS

A few all-natural additions to your standard first aid kit can help everything from a sunburn and bug bites to an upset tummy.

LAVENDER ESSENTIAL OIL

For sunburn, 30 drops in 1 ounce of coconut oil. Gently daub on to relieve the burn.

For bug bites, 15 to 20 drops in half an ounce of grapeseed oil. Apply directly to the bite area for relief.

BANANA PEEL

Believe it or not, bananas not only have healthy potassium, but the inside of the peel rubbed on a mosquito bite can stop the itching fast!

UPSET TUMMY

Settle an upset tummy with chamomile, peppermint, or ginger tea. Ginger also helps with motion or car sickness.

ALL-NATURAL BUG SPRAY

If you keep the bugs **off** you, they won't **bite** you! Try this great-smelling spray. In a spray bottle, mix:

- *2 ounces witch hazel*
- *2 ounces distilled water*
- *10 drops geranium essential oil*
- *15 drops lavender essential oil*
- *5 drops patchouli essential oil*
- *1 drop lemongrass essential oil*
- *10 drops citronella essential oil*

Shake well and spray on clothing and exposed-skin, avoiding the face and eye area.

PLANTS TO AVOID

Although it's called poison ivy, this irritating plant can be found growing on the ground and in the grass. Learning to identify the telltale three-leaf pattern is key! Look out for others like this too: poison oak and poison sumac.

poison ivy   *poison oak*   *poison sumac*

DATE: _____ LOCATION: _____

CAMPGROUND: _____ PHONE: _____

SITE #/ CABIN #: _____ COST PER NIGHT: _____

AMENITIES: _____

ELECTRIC: _____ WATER: _____ RESTROOMS: _____

WEATHER: _____

CAMPING COMPANIONS: _____

_____

_____

BEST MEALS: _____

_____

_____

FAVORITE MEMORIES: _____

_____

_____

_____

ADVENTURES AND SITES VISITED: _____

_____

_____

DATE: _____ LOCATION: _____

CAMPGROUND: _____ PHONE: _____

SITE #/ CABIN #: _____ COST PER NIGHT: _____

AMENITIES: _____

ELECTRIC: _____ WATER: _____ RESTROOMS: _____

WEATHER: _____

CAMPING COMPANIONS: _____

_____

_____

BEST MEALS: _____

_____

_____

FAVORITE MEMORIES: _____

_____

_____

_____

ADVENTURES AND SITES VISITED: _____

_____

_____

DATE: _____ LOCATION: _____

CAMPGROUND: _____ PHONE: _____

SITE #/ CABIN #: _____ COST PER NIGHT: _____

AMENITIES: _____

ELECTRIC: _____ WATER: _____ RESTROOMS: _____

WEATHER: _____

CAMPING COMPANIONS: _____

_____

_____

BEST MEALS: _____

_____

_____

FAVORITE MEMORIES: _____

_____

_____

_____

ADVENTURES AND SITES VISITED: _____

_____

_____

DATE: _____ LOCATION: _____

CAMPGROUND: _____ PHONE: _____

SITE #/ CABIN #: _____ COST PER NIGHT: _____

AMENITIES: _____

ELECTRIC: _____ WATER: _____ RESTROOMS: _____

WEATHER: _____

CAMPING COMPANIONS: _____
_____
_____

BEST MEALS: _____
_____
_____

FAVORITE MEMORIES: _____
_____
_____
_____

ADVENTURES AND SITES VISITED: _____
_____
_____

DATE: _____ LOCATION: _____

CAMPGROUND: _____ PHONE: _____

SITE #/ CABIN #: _____ COST PER NIGHT: _____

AMENITIES: _____

ELECTRIC: _____ WATER: _____ RESTROOMS: _____

WEATHER: _____

CAMPING COMPANIONS: _____
_____
_____

BEST MEALS: _____
_____
_____

FAVORITE MEMORIES: _____
_____
_____
_____

ADVENTURES AND SITES VISITED: _____
_____
_____

Bless the food before us,
the family beside us,
and the love between us.

AUTHOR UNKNOWN

KITCHEN
SUPPLIES

CAMP KITCHEN

Just as everyone gathers in the kitchen at home, the camp kitchen is where the action is! Simple or gourmet, a well-stocked kitchen is key to enjoying your camping adventures.

HOW TO PACK A COOLER

It seems simple, but there is really an art to packing a cooler! This layering technique helps food stay cooler longer and keeps your items much fresher.

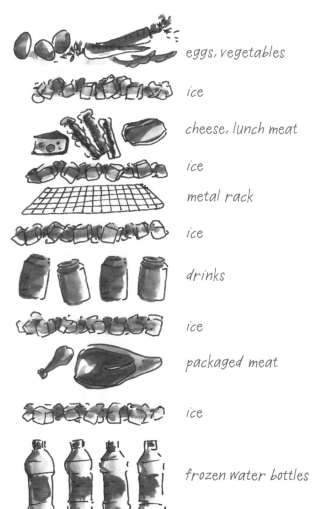

eggs, vegetables

ice

cheese, lunch meat

ice

metal rack

ice

drinks

ice

packaged meat

ice

frozen water bottles

KITCHEN ESSENTIALS

metal cup

cast-iron
Dutch oven

cast-iron pot

small cast-
iron pot

coffee pot

cast-iron pan

metal plates

wooden spoons

measuring spoons

metal cutlery

bottle opener

dish towels

plastic cutting boards

spatula

tongs

knives

can opener

corkscrew

peeler

hotdog forks

paper towels

aluminum foil

sponge

wash basin

pot holders
oven mitts

dish soap

DATE: _____ LOCATION: _____

CAMPGROUND: _____ PHONE: _____

SITE #/ CABIN #: _____ COST PER NIGHT: _____

AMENITIES: _____

ELECTRIC: _____ WATER: _____ RESTROOMS: _____

WEATHER: _____

CAMPING COMPANIONS: _____
_____
_____

BEST MEALS: _____
_____
_____

FAVORITE MEMORIES: _____
_____
_____
_____

ADVENTURES AND SITES VISITED: _____
_____
_____

DATE: _____ LOCATION: _____

CAMPGROUND: _____ PHONE: _____

SITE #/ CABIN #: _____ COST PER NIGHT: _____

AMENITIES: _____

ELECTRIC: _____ WATER: _____ RESTROOMS: _____

WEATHER: _____

CAMPING COMPANIONS: _____
_____
_____

BEST MEALS: _____
_____
_____

FAVORITE MEMORIES: _____
_____
_____
_____

ADVENTURES AND SITES VISITED: _____
_____
_____

DATE: _____ LOCATION: _____

CAMPGROUND: _____ PHONE: _____

SITE #/ CABIN #: _____ COST PER NIGHT: _____

AMENITIES: _____

ELECTRIC: _____ WATER: _____ RESTROOMS: _____

WEATHER: _____

CAMPING COMPANIONS: _____

_____

_____

BEST MEALS: _____

_____

_____

FAVORITE MEMORIES: _____

_____

_____

_____

ADVENTURES AND SITES VISITED: _____

_____

_____

DATE: _____ LOCATION: _____

CAMPGROUND: _____ PHONE: _____

SITE #/ CABIN #: _____ COST PER NIGHT: _____

AMENITIES: _____

ELECTRIC: _____ WATER: _____ RESTROOMS: _____

WEATHER: _____

CAMPING COMPANIONS: _____

_____

_____

BEST MEALS: _____

_____

_____

FAVORITE MEMORIES: _____

_____

_____

_____

ADVENTURES AND SITES VISITED: _____

_____

_____

DATE: _____ LOCATION: _____

CAMPGROUND: _____ PHONE: _____

SITE #/ CABIN #: _____ COST PER NIGHT: _____

AMENITIES: _____

ELECTRIC: _____ WATER: _____ RESTROOMS: _____

WEATHER: _____

CAMPING COMPANIONS: _____
_____
_____

BEST MEALS: _____
_____
_____

FAVORITE MEMORIES: _____
_____
_____
_____

ADVENTURES AND SITES VISITED: _____
_____
_____

The chief pleasure
in eating does not consist
in costly seasoning,
or exquisite flavor,
but in yourself.

HORACE

EATING WELL

ON THE CAMP MENU

Cooking meals over an open fire or on a camp stove puts the heart into the whole camping experience. From s'mores to a tasty dinner, ideas for making delicious food under the stars are endless.

BREAKFAST

CINNAMON ROLLS ON A STICK

Crack open a package of cinnamon rolls and wrap each one around a stick. Toast over the fire until done and golden brown. Transfer to a plate and add icing.

MAKE-AHEAD BREAKFAST BURRITOS

At home, cook up eggs, bacon or sausage, onions, and peppers. Season to taste. Put any ingredients you like on a tortilla and add shredded cheese. Wrap up in foil and freeze.

When camping, let the foil-wrapped burrito thaw and then put it in hot coals. Everything is already cooked. You're just heating it up and melting the cheese.

FOIL PACKET DINNERS

These dinners are so good and easy, you will want to make them at home too! Just layer the ingredients in foil, wrap up, and cook via your campfire.

top layer: evoo, wine, or lemon juice

layer 2: seasoned meat

layer 1: seasoned veggies

foil

The first layer is chopped veggies, salt/pepper/spices/herbs, and olive oil. The next layer is seasoned meat. The top layer is just a splash of olive oil, wine, or lemon juice. Wrap up the packet and cook over a fire. The cooking time will vary depending on the heat of your fire and the meat you are using.

shrimp	chicken	steak	evoo
squash	chopped onion	mushrooms	herbs
asparagus	broccoli	carrots	salt +
chopped pepper	corn	chopped onion	pepper
zucchini	squash	sliced potatoes	

DESSERTS

S'MORES

We all know the classic version, but these sweet treats are fantastic with just a few changes! Instead of graham crackers, fill a waffle cone with mini marshmallows and chocolate chips. Wrap in foil and put into hot coals to toast and melt.

Or you can add sliced strawberries to the classic s'more.

S'MORE BANANAS!

Make a slit in a banana peel and slice the banana into coins, leaving in the peel. Add mini marshmallows, graham cracker pieces, and chocolate chips. Wrap in foil and tuck into the coals until the chocolate is nice and melty.

APPLE CRISP

In a mixing bowl, add some oats, brown sugar, a pinch or two of flour, cinnamon, and butter pieces. Stir with a fork until the mixture resembles coarse crumbs. On a foil square, sprinkle the mixture over chopped apple slices. Fold into a pouch and tuck into hot coals to cook.

DATE: _____ LOCATION: _____

CAMPGROUND: _____ PHONE: _____

SITE #/ CABIN #: _____ COST PER NIGHT: _____

AMENITIES: _____

ELECTRIC: _____ WATER: _____ RESTROOMS: _____

WEATHER: _____

CAMPING COMPANIONS: _____
_____
_____

BEST MEALS: _____
_____
_____

FAVORITE MEMORIES: _____
_____
_____
_____

ADVENTURES AND SITES VISITED: _____
_____
_____

DATE: _____ LOCATION: _____

CAMPGROUND: _____ PHONE: _____

SITE #/ CABIN #: _____ COST PER NIGHT: _____

AMENITIES: _____

ELECTRIC: _____ WATER: _____ RESTROOMS: _____

WEATHER: _____

CAMPING COMPANIONS: _____

_____

_____

BEST MEALS: _____

_____

_____

FAVORITE MEMORIES: _____

_____

_____

_____

ADVENTURES AND SITES VISITED: _____

_____

_____

DATE: _____ LOCATION: _____

CAMPGROUND: _____ PHONE: _____

SITE #/ CABIN #: _____ COST PER NIGHT: _____

AMENITIES: _____

ELECTRIC: _____ WATER: _____ RESTROOMS: _____

WEATHER: _____

CAMPING COMPANIONS: _____

_____

_____

BEST MEALS: _____

_____

_____

FAVORITE MEMORIES: _____

_____

_____

_____

ADVENTURES AND SITES VISITED: _____

_____

_____

DATE: _____ LOCATION: _____

CAMPGROUND: _____ PHONE: _____

SITE #/ CABIN #: _____ COST PER NIGHT: _____

AMENITIES: _____

ELECTRIC: _____ WATER: _____ RESTROOMS: _____

WEATHER: _____

CAMPING COMPANIONS: _____

_____

_____

BEST MEALS: _____

_____

_____

FAVORITE MEMORIES: _____

_____

_____

_____

ADVENTURES AND SITES VISITED: _____

_____

_____

DATE: _____ LOCATION: _____

CAMPGROUND: _____ PHONE: _____

SITE #/ CABIN #: _____ COST PER NIGHT: _____

AMENITIES: _____

ELECTRIC: _____ WATER: _____ RESTROOMS: _____

WEATHER: _____

CAMPING COMPANIONS: _____
_____
_____

BEST MEALS: _____
_____
_____

FAVORITE MEMORIES: _____
_____
_____
_____

ADVENTURES AND SITES VISITED: _____
_____
_____

The power of finding beauty
in the humblest things
makes home happy
and life lovely.

LOUISA MAY ALCOTT

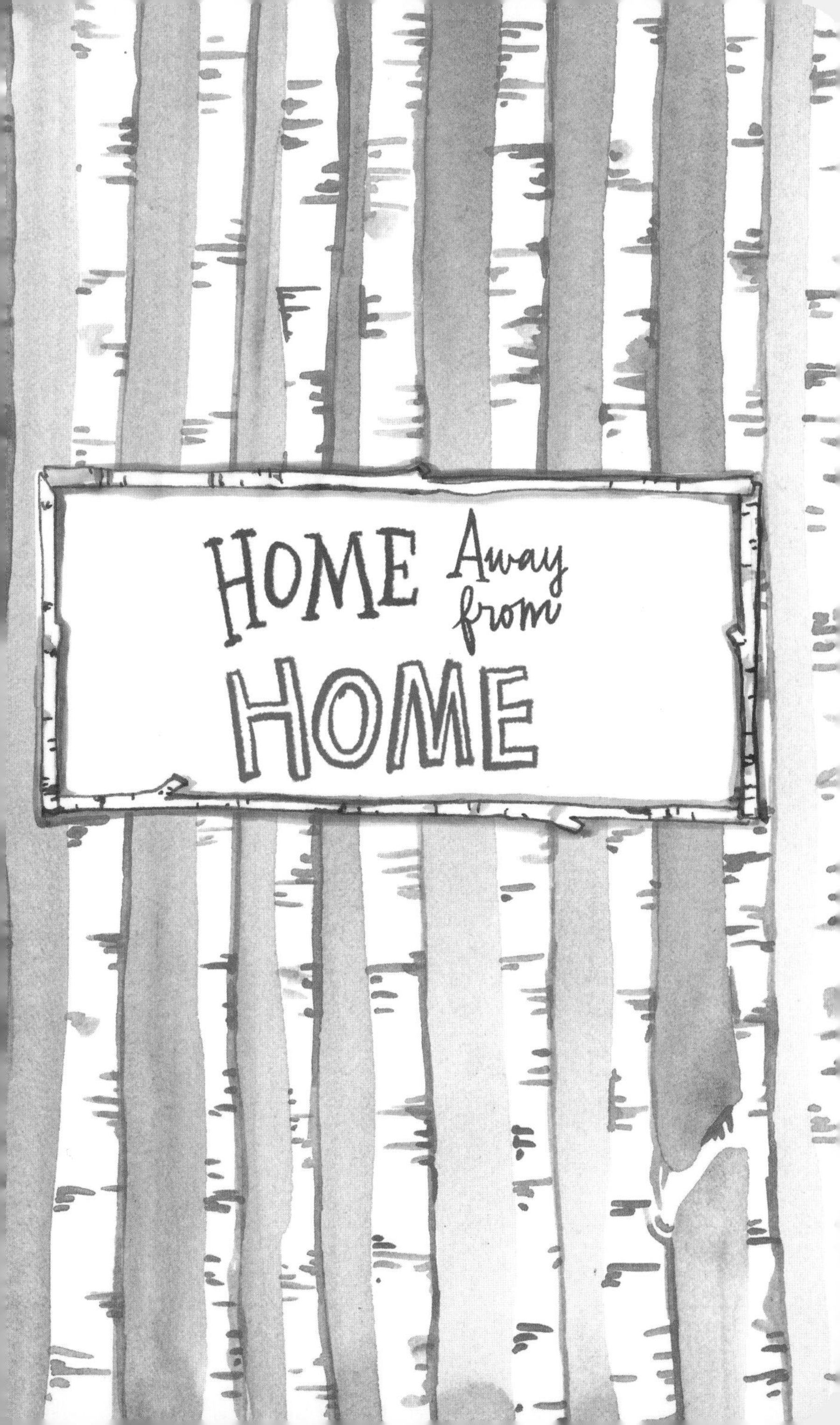
HOME Away from HOME

CAMPSITE

The perfect campsite can make all the difference in any nature adventure. Whether you're sleeping under the stars or in a fancy RV, it's the views, the friends, and the stories you remember when you're gathered around the campfire.

74

GIVE ME SHELTER

MY HUMBLE ABODE
Basic tarp, rope, and stakes

THE STUDIO
Small pup tent

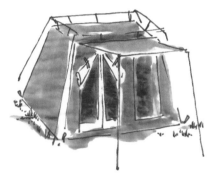

FRONT PORCH COTTAGE
One- to two-room tent with an awning

TWENTY-FIRST-CENTURY NOMAD
Pull-behind trailer

MY MOBILE PENTHOUSE
Lap of luxury RV

BUILDING YOUR CAMPFIRE

The way to build a successful campfire is related to the size of the wood. Start with **tinder** (little twigs the length of your hand). Then add **kindling** (small sticks no thicker than your thumb). Lastly, add **fuel** (wood no thinner than your wrist).

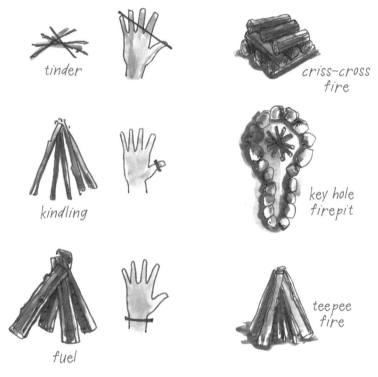

tinder

criss-cross fire

kindling

key hole firepit

fuel

teepee fire

Just as important as building a campfire is knowing the proper way to extinguish one. **Drown, stir**, and **feel.** Drown the fire with water, use a shovel to stir it up and smother it with dirt, and, lastly, feel the dirt. If it's hot, it's not out. Repeat the steps.

CAMPER'S PRAYER

For the land that we travel,
and the stars high above.
For campfires so bright,
and for all those we love.

We thank you, O Lord, for
the world we explore.
Please keep us and guide us
through this land we adore.
Amen.

DATE: _____ LOCATION: _____

CAMPGROUND: _____ PHONE: _____

SITE #/ CABIN #: _____ COST PER NIGHT: _____

AMENITIES: _____

ELECTRIC: _____ WATER: _____ RESTROOMS: _____

WEATHER: _____

CAMPING COMPANIONS: _____
_____
_____

BEST MEALS: _____
_____
_____

FAVORITE MEMORIES: _____
_____
_____
_____

ADVENTURES AND SITES VISITED: _____
_____
_____

DATE: _____ LOCATION: _____

CAMPGROUND: _____ PHONE: _____

SITE #/ CABIN #: _____ COST PER NIGHT: _____

AMENITIES: _____

ELECTRIC: _____ WATER: _____ RESTROOMS: _____

WEATHER: _____

CAMPING COMPANIONS: _____

_____

_____

BEST MEALS: _____

_____

_____

FAVORITE MEMORIES: _____

_____

_____

_____

ADVENTURES AND SITES VISITED: _____

_____

_____

DATE: _____ LOCATION: _____

CAMPGROUND: _____ PHONE: _____

SITE #/ CABIN #: _____ COST PER NIGHT: _____

AMENITIES: _____

ELECTRIC: _____ WATER: _____ RESTROOMS: _____

WEATHER: _____

CAMPING COMPANIONS: _____

_____

_____

BEST MEALS: _____

_____

_____

FAVORITE MEMORIES: _____

_____

_____

_____

ADVENTURES AND SITES VISITED: _____

_____

_____

DATE: _____ LOCATION: _____

CAMPGROUND: _____ PHONE: _____

SITE #/ CABIN #: _____ COST PER NIGHT: _____

AMENITIES: _____

ELECTRIC: _____ WATER: _____ RESTROOMS: _____

WEATHER: _____

CAMPING COMPANIONS: _____
_____
_____

BEST MEALS: _____
_____
_____

FAVORITE MEMORIES: _____
_____
_____
_____

ADVENTURES AND SITES VISITED: _____
_____
_____

DATE: _____ LOCATION: _____

CAMPGROUND: _____ PHONE: _____

SITE #/ CABIN #: _____ COST PER NIGHT: _____

AMENITIES: _____

ELECTRIC: _____ WATER: _____ RESTROOMS: _____

WEATHER: _____

CAMPING COMPANIONS: _____

_____

_____

BEST MEALS: _____

_____

_____

FAVORITE MEMORIES: _____

_____

_____

_____

ADVENTURES AND SITES VISITED: _____

_____

_____

*Life is more fun
if you play games.*

ROALD DAHL

CAMP FUN

Camping is all about fun, and it doesn't take much to make some great family memories. There are always classic outdoor games such as horseshoes, bocce ball, Frisbee, and Cornhole. However, with a little bit of DIY creativity, you can make some fun new games the kids will enjoy making as much as playing.

OUTDOOR GAMES

LAWN DICE

Paint dice dots on cardboard boxes. (The boxes
can fold flat to save space when not in use.)
One way to use the dice is in a game
of Simon Says: "Four tiny steps,"
"Three bunny hops," etc.

BEANBAG TOSS

Use paper plates with points written
on them for a beanbag toss.

TIC-TAC-TOE

A simple tic-tac-toe can be made
from sticks, stones, and acorns.

RING TOSS

An inflatable pool ring and a wooden
stake easily make a ring toss.

ANIMAL TRACKS

One of the most fun things to do when out on a hike is to check for animal tracks. Deer are easy to spot, but look out for the skunk!

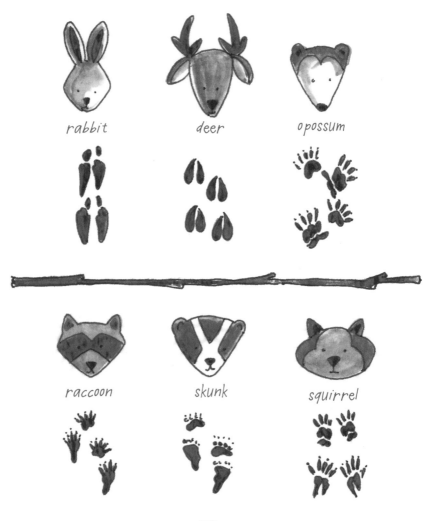

rabbit   deer   opossum

raccoon   skunk   squirrel

FATHER ABRAHAM

Father Abraham had many sons
Many sons had Father Abraham
I am one of them, and so are you
So let's all praise the Lord
Right arm!

(swing right arm) (Repeat verse)

Right arm! Left arm!

(swing right arm and left arm) (Repeat verse)

Right arm! Left arm! Right foot!

(swing both arms and step with right foot) (Repeat verse)

Right arm! Left arm! Right foot! Left foot!

(swing both arms and march in place) (Repeat verse)

Right arm! Left arm! Right foot!
Left foot! Chin up!

(swing both arms and march in place with chin up)
(Repeat verse)

Right arm! Left arm! Right foot! Left foot!
Chin up! Turn around!

(swing both arms and march in place with chin up
and turn around) (Repeat verse)

Right arm! Left arm! Right foot! Left foot!
Chin up! Turn around! Sit down!

(swing both arms and march in place with chin up
and turn around and sit down)

DATE: _____ LOCATION: _____

CAMPGROUND: _____ PHONE: _____

SITE #/ CABIN #: _____ COST PER NIGHT: _____

AMENITIES: _____

ELECTRIC: _____ WATER: _____ RESTROOMS: _____

WEATHER: _____

CAMPING COMPANIONS: _____
_____
_____

BEST MEALS: _____
_____
_____

FAVORITE MEMORIES: _____
_____
_____
_____

ADVENTURES AND SITES VISITED: _____
_____
_____

DATE: _____ LOCATION: _____

CAMPGROUND: _____ PHONE: _____

SITE #/ CABIN #: _____ COST PER NIGHT: _____

AMENITIES: _____

ELECTRIC: _____ WATER: _____ RESTROOMS: _____

WEATHER: _____

CAMPING COMPANIONS: _____

_____

_____

BEST MEALS: _____

_____

_____

FAVORITE MEMORIES: _____

_____

_____

_____

ADVENTURES AND SITES VISITED: _____

_____

_____

DATE: _____ LOCATION: _____

CAMPGROUND: _____ PHONE: _____

SITE #/ CABIN #: _____ COST PER NIGHT: _____

AMENITIES: _____

ELECTRIC: _____ WATER: _____ RESTROOMS: _____

WEATHER: _____

CAMPING COMPANIONS: _____

_____

_____

BEST MEALS: _____

_____

_____

FAVORITE MEMORIES: _____

_____

_____

_____

ADVENTURES AND SITES VISITED: _____

_____

_____

DATE: _____ LOCATION: _____

CAMPGROUND: _____ PHONE: _____

SITE #/ CABIN #: _____ COST PER NIGHT: _____

AMENITIES: _____

ELECTRIC: _____ WATER: _____ RESTROOMS: _____

WEATHER: _____

CAMPING COMPANIONS: _____
_____
_____

BEST MEALS: _____
_____
_____

FAVORITE MEMORIES: _____
_____
_____
_____

ADVENTURES AND SITES VISITED: _____
_____
_____

DATE: _____ LOCATION: _____

CAMPGROUND: _____ PHONE: _____

SITE #/ CABIN #: _____ COST PER NIGHT: _____

AMENITIES: _____

ELECTRIC: _____ WATER: _____ RESTROOMS: _____

WEATHER: _____

CAMPING COMPANIONS: _____
_____
_____

BEST MEALS: _____
_____
_____

FAVORITE MEMORIES: _____
_____
_____
_____

ADVENTURES AND SITES VISITED: _____
_____
_____

Glamping—the best way to
have s'more fun!

MICHAL SPARKS

GLAMPING

GLAMOROUS +
CAMPING = GLAMPING

Glamping isn't just for music festivals anymore. It's for all of us who enjoy a deluxe getaway. Flowers on the table; a rug on the ground; linens, dishes, gourmet treats, and some tunes from your phone. Really, it's just about making your experience as comfortable and glamorous as you would like...and why not? You deserve the best!

THE COMFORTS OF HOME

You have to bring these items when camping, so why not make them beautiful? Outdoor dinnerware has come a long way. Melamine dishes are both beautiful and durable, and melamine stemware looks just like glass. Add a floor covering to your tent—many outdoor mats resemble Persian carpets! Add chic folding chairs and soft lighting, and before you know it, you are glamping!

melamine stemware

lanterns

melamine dishes and linens

chic folding chairs

candles (real flame or battery operated)

outdoor floor coverings

throws and blankets

THE GLAMOROUS GRILL

Elevate a simple shish kebab with olive oil, sea salt, and brussels sprouts roasted low and slow. Or consider heirloom tomatoes with pesto chicken pieces, or herbed shrimp, brushed with lemon, butter, and wine.

An easy appetizer is a wheel of Brie with spiced pine nuts on top, wrapped in foil and warmed over the fire until soft. Serve with bread or crackers.

Keep things simple with a gourmet cheese board. Or a selection of figs, pears, grapes, berries, olives, and nuts with assorted meats and cheeses. Sundried tomatoes, olive tapenade, pesto spread and spicy mustard are also delicious. Whichever you choose, add some crusty bread with olive oil for dipping and sea salt for sprinkling!

Use your cheese board goodies to make gourmet sandwiches. How about pear, prosciutto, and Brie, or maybe prosciutto, pesto, and sundried tomatoes with mozzarella? Or olive tapenade, sliced figs, cheese, and crusty bread! The combinations are endless!

THE SOPHISTICATED S'MORE

For those who love the idea of an elegant campfire-toasted dessert, the strawberry s'more is the perfect glamor treat. Place a chocolate-covered strawberry on a skewer, dip it in marshmallow fluff, and then toast it.

FRENCH PRESS— DON'T LEAVE HOME WITHOUT IT!

After a gourmet evening, what better way to wake up but with a cup of French-pressed coffee? Truly a camping must-have, the French press makes the best cup of java and only needs boiling water and ground coffee. Bring the experience to the next level with a coffee frother—a simple, inexpensive, battery-operated whisk that blends cream into your coffee in the most delicious way!

DATE: _____ LOCATION: _____

CAMPGROUND: _____ PHONE: _____

SITE #/ CABIN #: _____ COST PER NIGHT: _____

AMENITIES: _____

ELECTRIC: _____ WATER: _____ RESTROOMS: _____

WEATHER: _____

CAMPING COMPANIONS: _____

_____

_____

BEST MEALS: _____

_____

_____

FAVORITE MEMORIES: _____

_____

_____

_____

ADVENTURES AND SITES VISITED: _____

_____

_____

DATE: _____ LOCATION: _____

CAMPGROUND: _____ PHONE: _____

SITE #/ CABIN #: _____ COST PER NIGHT: _____

AMENITIES: _____

ELECTRIC: _____ WATER: _____ RESTROOMS: _____

WEATHER: _____

CAMPING COMPANIONS: _____

_____

_____

BEST MEALS: _____

_____

_____

FAVORITE MEMORIES: _____

_____

_____

_____

ADVENTURES AND SITES VISITED: _____

_____

_____

DATE: _____ LOCATION: _____

CAMPGROUND: _____ PHONE: _____

SITE #/ CABIN #: _____ COST PER NIGHT: _____

AMENITIES: _____

ELECTRIC: _____ WATER: _____ RESTROOMS: _____

WEATHER: _____

CAMPING COMPANIONS: _____

_____

_____

BEST MEALS: _____

_____

_____

FAVORITE MEMORIES: _____

_____

_____

_____

ADVENTURES AND SITES VISITED: _____

_____

_____

DATE: _____ LOCATION: _____

CAMPGROUND: _____ PHONE: _____

SITE #/ CABIN #: _____ COST PER NIGHT: _____

AMENITIES: _____

ELECTRIC: _____ WATER: _____ RESTROOMS: _____

WEATHER: _____

CAMPING COMPANIONS: _____
_____
_____

BEST MEALS: _____
_____
_____

FAVORITE MEMORIES: _____
_____
_____
_____

ADVENTURES AND SITES VISITED: _____
_____
_____

DATE: _____ LOCATION: _____

CAMPGROUND: _____ PHONE: _____

SITE #/ CABIN #: _____ COST PER NIGHT: _____

AMENITIES: _____

ELECTRIC: _____ WATER: _____ RESTROOMS: _____

WEATHER: _____

CAMPING COMPANIONS: _____
_____
_____

BEST MEALS: _____
_____
_____

FAVORITE MEMORIES: _____
_____
_____
_____

ADVENTURES AND SITES VISITED: _____
_____
_____

In his hand are the
depths of the earth,
and the mountain peaks
belong to him.

PSALM 95:4

REVELING in NATURE

THE GREAT OUTDOORS

Experiencing the great outdoors…it's why we camp. Whether we're hiking in the woods, paddling across a lake, or snapping the perfect photo, being in nature revives our senses, relieves stress, and provides a different point of view. And it's all about the view!

ON THE TRAIL—BE COMFORTABLE, SAFE, AND PREPARED

backpack

canvas hat

pack a backpack

light

heavy   light

medium

sleeping bag

water bottle

mini first aid kit

extra socks

nut snacks

rain poncho

sunscreen

bug spray

hiking boots

ON THE WATER—BE COMFORTABLE, SAFE, AND PREPARED

life jacket

compass

extra paddle

water bottle

mini first aid kit

multipurpose knife

energy bars

rain poncho

BRINGING NATURE HOME

Being able to record experiences when out in nature is one way to bring your camping trip home. Nature photography is a wonderful way to capture a moment or a view you never want to forget.

Keeping an art journal to record a moment is easily done with watercolor pencils. Sketch on sight and add water later to make the sketch become a painting. Also, use your photos for painting inspiration after you get home.

Bird-watching is a fun way to become involved in the nature of the region. Make sure to have a guide to the birds of the area you'll be visiting.

DATE: _____ LOCATION: _____

CAMPGROUND: _____ PHONE: _____

SITE #/ CABIN #: _____ COST PER NIGHT: _____

AMENITIES: _____

ELECTRIC: _____ WATER: _____ RESTROOMS: _____

WEATHER: _____

CAMPING COMPANIONS: _____

_____

_____

BEST MEALS: _____

_____

_____

FAVORITE MEMORIES: _____

_____

_____

_____

ADVENTURES AND SITES VISITED: _____

_____

_____

DATE: _____ LOCATION: _____

CAMPGROUND: _____ PHONE: _____

SITE #/ CABIN #: _____ COST PER NIGHT: _____

AMENITIES: _____

ELECTRIC: _____ WATER: _____ RESTROOMS: _____

WEATHER: _____

CAMPING COMPANIONS: _____

_____

_____

BEST MEALS: _____

_____

_____

FAVORITE MEMORIES: _____

_____

_____

_____

ADVENTURES AND SITES VISITED: _____

_____

_____

DATE: _____ LOCATION: _____

CAMPGROUND: _____ PHONE: _____

SITE #/ CABIN #: _____ COST PER NIGHT: _____

AMENITIES: _____

ELECTRIC: _____ WATER: _____ RESTROOMS: _____

WEATHER: _____

CAMPING COMPANIONS: _____

_____

_____

BEST MEALS: _____

_____

_____

FAVORITE MEMORIES: _____

_____

_____

_____

ADVENTURES AND SITES VISITED: _____

_____

_____

DATE: _____ LOCATION: _____

CAMPGROUND: _____ PHONE: _____

SITE #/ CABIN #: _____ COST PER NIGHT: _____

AMENITIES: _____

ELECTRIC: _____ WATER: _____ RESTROOMS: _____

WEATHER: _____

CAMPING COMPANIONS: _____

_____

_____

BEST MEALS: _____

_____

_____

FAVORITE MEMORIES: _____

_____

_____

_____

ADVENTURES AND SITES VISITED: _____

_____

_____

DATE: _____ LOCATION: _____

CAMPGROUND: _____ PHONE: _____

SITE #/ CABIN #: _____ COST PER NIGHT: _____

AMENITIES: _____

ELECTRIC: _____ WATER: _____ RESTROOMS: _____

WEATHER: _____

CAMPING COMPANIONS: _____

_____

_____

BEST MEALS: _____

_____

_____

FAVORITE MEMORIES: _____

_____

_____

_____

ADVENTURES AND SITES VISITED: _____

_____

_____

Do what you can,
with what you have,
where you are.

THEODORE ROOSEVELT